◆ FriesenPress

Suite 300 - 990 Fort St
Victoria, BC, V8V 3K2
Canada

www.friesenpress.com

To contact Yalda Kazemi for speaking arrangements or events please email info@stylesteem.ca or visit www.stylesteem.ca

ISBN
978-1-03-910496-9 (Hardcover)
978-1-03-910495-2 (Paperback)
78-1-03-910497-6 (eBook)

1. SELF HELP, MOOD DISORDERS, MENTAL HEALTH

Distributed to the trade by The Ingram Book Company

UNAPOLOGETIC TRUTHS

THE REALITIES OF POSTPARTUM
WE DON'T TALK ABOUT

YALDA KAZEMI

Dedicated firstly to my son, Amir.
You are forever my heart and soul.

And to all the individuals who have lost their voices
and are suffering in silence, you are not alone, and
you will be yourself again.

TABLE OF
CONTENTS

PREFACE

No one could have prepared me for what was to come.

I had heard every possible story about the difficulties and hardships of pregnancy and labour. The horror stories about birth, which to be frank, petrified me, but I was somewhat prepared nonetheless.

Yet the days, weeks, and months that followed the birth of my son proved to be very different than what I expected.

This book is first and foremost about resiliency, hope, and the importance of help and support. It is a book about victory, empowerment, strength, courage, and confidence.

I write this narrative of my severe battle and ultimate victory over postpartum mental illness in hopes that it will help those who are currently experiencing, may one day be faced with, or supporting an individual battling with this ailment or other forms of mental illness.

Although I predominantly focus on postpartum mental illness, please know that the topics and strategies I discuss in this book can pertain and are relevant to anyone experiencing depression or anxiety.

I not only focus on the hardships associated with mental illness, but the positivity that results from it as well. I want individuals who have never experienced symptoms of depression, anxiety, or psychosis first-hand to understand what they actually feel like.

My intention is to help you understand what takes place in the mind and body of someone suffering with these ailments. To know what is thought and felt—the utter and complete depths of despair, hopelessness, and loneliness that they experience.

I also explain how to overcome all of that negativity, discuss how the journey is filled with both ups and downs, and highlight the positivity that can result from the experience.

The intent of sharing my story is not to scare you, but to help you understand how to deal with mental illness and how to heal.

Let me be clear at the outset: it is extremely rare to be sick with postpartum mental illness for the duration that I was. There were many factors that contributed to my remaining ill for so long—biological factors, unnecessary external stressors, self-imposed negligence, and just some plain bad luck. But I want to be clear that most who experience this ailment will heal in a much shorter period of time. So please, don't feel hopeless; there is indeed a light at the end of this tunnel.

Often, people use the statement "ignorance is bliss" loosely. But in this instance, ignorance was my downfall. Awareness, knowledge, understanding, and patience will allow you or your loved ones to heal.

I wrote this book with the hope that the next mother suffering as I did doesn't feel hopeless and alone. I want her to know that it is absolutely okay, and in fact, encouraged, to ask for help.

I want her to know that she is immensely strong and courageous despite her illness and mind trying to convince her otherwise.

But most importantly, I want her to know that she will be herself again.

I've intentionally kept this book short because I know that a depressed and anxious mind doesn't have the patience for reading. However, I also know first-hand how much the mind wants to find solace in knowing it's not alone.

I want this book to explain the journey, relationships, misconceptions, hindering processes, recovery, and support strategies that will help with healing. But I wish to do so in a real, authentic, unapologetic, and unfiltered way from the perspective of a mother and a woman who endured it all and overcame it.

Postpartum mental illness is not new, and it is not uncommon. However, it is often not spoken about due to all of the shame, judgement, guilt, embarrassment, fear, and stigma associated with it.

My mission is to raise awareness and be a voice for all the mothers out there who are suffering in silence.

I hope that sharing my story and experience will aid in your journey to becoming YOU again.

This book is also a symbol of celebration for me. Celebrating my ability to love my child and feel connected to him. Celebrating the ability to articulate, think, write, and carry on with conversations again. Celebrating strength, courage, and resiliency. Celebrating the fact that I am myself again.

I leave you with a quote from a speech I provided at an awareness and fundraising initiative in support of perinatal mental health:

> My husband once mentioned to me, postpartum mental illness knows no prejudice. It can affect any mother regardless of race, age, or socioeconomic status. He was right. At the end of the day, we all came from a woman, we all know a woman, and whether it's you, your mother, sister, friend, aunt, cousin, partner, co-worker, or any woman in your life, she may have been, may currently be, or may one day go through something like I did and need the support necessary to overcome mental illness and feel whole again.

I hope this book helps you or your loved ones through your journey and recovery process.

With love,
Yalda

1
LET'S BEGIN

He's real.

He exists.

He is my reason for being.

I know this now, but there was a time when it all felt like a figment of my imagination. A time when I doubted my own existence and thought the world around me was a dream. Lost, sad, unmotivated, anxious, petrified, delusional, confused, and empty: a few of the words describing how I felt after I gave birth to my son, Amir, in 2013. Not all the words were immediately fitting, but in the days and months that would come to pass, these and more would become ways to describe me. The always-motivated, ambitious, high-achieving person that I knew was no longer there.

All that was left was the feeling that I was a soulless, empty shell—a person dead on the inside, walking and existing, albeit barely, among the living. That was me for the nearly two and a half years it took to finally be "normal" again.

To finally be ME again. But would I change any of it now? No.

Although the experience was the most horrific and troubling period of my life, I'm actually grateful for what I endured.

It gave me a second chance at life.

It made me change who I am for the better and tremendously

altered my perspective on life, relationships, and overall happiness.

But most importantly, I believe that it made me truly appreciate my love for my son even more than I could have otherwise.

It has made my bond and love for Amir the most remarkable and amazing feeling I have ever felt.

No words can adequately describe the intensity by which I love him.

During my illness, people often described my eyes as blank, empty, and lifeless, stating that the person they knew was no longer there.

Amir is the life that has now returned to my eyes.

He is now the soul that was once missing.

∞∞∞

Postpartum mental illness took so much from me.

It robbed me of my son's early years and my ability to fully and adequately experience motherhood for the first two years.

Years and moments that I will never get back.

Although I was physically present, there are moments and important milestones from his infancy that I have absolutely no recollection of.

I rely on stories, recollections, and images that were shared with me by my family and friends to relive those moments.

I often used to sit with other moms who reminisced about the first time their children sat up, ate solids, crawled, spoke their first words, and took their first steps.

I used to sit there and smile.

I smiled to stop myself from crying.

Crying because unlike them, I don't remember many of those moments from my son's life.

Postpartum mental illness took all of that from me.

But you know what?

It actually gave me so much more in return.

The ability to truly understand and feel the unconditional love between my son and I.

The ability to wholly experience love and happiness and be grateful for it.

The ability to be courageous, strong, and resilient—more so than I could have ever imagined.

Because now, the way I look at it, postpartum mental illness didn't destroy me, so no other life obstacle or person can.

It helped me fuel the fire of motivation and ambition. The desire to achieve all of my goals.

Because I now know that I can!

It led me to be grateful for every day that I have. For every day on earth and every day with those I love, particularly my son.

It took away my negative and pessimistic perceptions about life and led me on a path to understanding that positivity can always arise from negative experiences.

Life is not always fair or happy, but how we choose to interpret a situation and how we overcome it is our choice.

What we do with our lives after a negative experience is our choice.

Postpartum mental illness gave me some of the greatest gifts in life: the appreciation of what unconditional love brings into our lives, a renewed sense of self-love, purpose, and gratitude.

For that, I will be eternally thankful.

ooooo

The final words I heard just before the doctor delivered my son were, "You will now feel some pressure."

Just like that, he was here. This tiny little human, my baby. My son, Amir.

But the moment he arrived, I felt a sudden spark, almost a jolt of electricity, rushing through my head.

I remember closing my eyes and opening them again, and all I could do was look into space and feel an overwhelming sense of emptiness.

A complete feeling of detachment, confusion, and emotionless—the exact opposite of the loving, tearful, joyous images that television shows and other moms had led me to anticipate.

I remember tilting my head back and looking at my husband, Kaveh, as he laid eyes on our son.

He was beaming with joy, his eyes filled with the very tears of happiness I expected to have. But me, nothing.

anxious, and the symptoms of depression continued.

At this point, I analyzed my feelings and thoughts almost obsessively.

I started overanalyzing my symptoms and progress and constantly looked for signs of improvement or continued deterioration.

This need to analyze myself became so intense that eventually, I started to exhibit symptoms of Obsessive-Compulsive Disorder (OCD) as well.

As if I didn't already have enough to deal with, why not add another diagnosis into the mix?

I try and add some humour to the experience now, but let me be blunt; it was anything but humorous when I was actually going through all of it.

By this point, my symptoms of anxiety overpowered the depressive ones.

I experienced so much anxiety that I was utterly and completely afraid of being left alone with my son.

Every single day that my husband had to go to work, I felt as though my world was falling apart.

The mere thought of spending those hours alone with Amir shook me to my core.

The fear was so intense that my family or close friends had to be with me in order to make it through the day.

On the days that they couldn't be there, I immediately left the house and went to the local malls.

I put Amir in a stroller, and I walked or sat around the mall for hours.

I fed him in the stroller and put him to sleep in it. There was no routine or real structure—I just focused on survival. Kept my son alive. Made it through the day until Kaveh or my mom, Soraya, got home from work, survived the rest of the evening, and tried to fall asleep at night.

That was my daily mission.

Just survive.

But let's be honest; that was an unrealistic expectation to place on myself as well as my family and friends.

Yes, they loved and cared for me, but they had their own lives, jobs, and responsibilities.

They couldn't be at my beck and call every single day just because I was afraid to be alone with my child and my thoughts.

Get a grip on yourself, Yalda. You can't expect someone to be around you all the time. You have to learn to be alone with your child.

I repeated those words to myself every day and night.

But like I said before, an anxious and depressed mind can't easily rationalize or grasp common sense.

So often, the fear and anxiety overpowered me.

Bless the ones who were there for me during that time; despite having their own lives, they came.

They worked around their commitments and made me and Amir a priority.

They stayed with me, even if it was for only a few hours a day, so that I could feel slightly calmer and a little bit of relief from my anxiety.

Individuals like my mom and sisters, Ayda and Donya, would take turns sleeping over to help me and Kaveh with nightly baby feedings in an effort to allow us to get a few hours of sleep.

Bless them, the ones who took the time to understand what I was going through and helped me through the journey instead of judging me as others did.

For those of you who do not have the support of family or friends, please know that support doesn't have to come from these traditional support groups.

There are many sources of support, such as your doctor, counsellors, postpartum and mom support groups who can help you through this experience.

Don't give up.

My anxiety was so paralyzing that I remember being afraid to sleep.

Afraid because sleep was not only difficult and hard to do, but it was my only solace away from it all.

It was the only moment in time when I didn't feel like I was about to hyperventilate, throw up, or cry.

The only moment when I felt that I could breathe and wanted to continue living.

I started to fear sleeping because after I woke up, I would have to experience the soul-crushing anxiety and sadness all over again the following day.

That fear haunted me.

Each night, I went to bed with the fear of knowing that tomorrow wouldn't necessarily be a better day.

In fact, some days were even worse than the previous ones, but I had to endure it over and over again.

So many nights, I remember wishing that I would never wake again so the suffering would stop.

Don't get me wrong, the anxiety still continued throughout the day as well. But when my people were around me, it was more bearable, and I could survive.

Not fully function, but survive.

Amid all of this, as though the agony I was experiencing weren't enough, I also dealt with the pressures of others and their unsolicited and unwanted comments about my parenting and the lack of routine for my child.

Judgements about why he was not eating and sleeping at a set time, in a set location, and so on and so forth.

I'll delve into this a lot more in Chapter Three.

But for now, let me tell you this . . . who cares what others think?

There is no right way.

When you're going through anxiety and depression, *survival* is the right way.

Doing what you need to in order to keep your child and yourself healthy and alive is the right way.

As long as you're meeting your baby's needs and helping your child flourish, you don't need to worry about adhering to anyone else's standards.

You need to be flexible and remove unnecessary expectations from yourself in order to heal.

It doesn't matter if your child doesn't sleep or eat at a set time every day.

It doesn't matter if they don't sleep at home in their crib, but a stroller or car seat as you try your best to make it through the day.

In the grand scheme of things, routine won't matter as much as doing what you need to in order to get the medical attention you need and work toward becoming healthy again.

Don't get me wrong, routines and schedules are great to have if you can, and they may be a necessary component for some of you in order to survive.

But if you can't initially adhere to them and routines don't necessarily work for you, then stop trying to force them into place.

Focus on meeting your baby's daily needs and improving your health.

Once you've healed, you can get to a point where you create and adhere to set routines and schedules.

Focus on healing, because you can't adequately help your child if you aren't well yourself.

You may be physically present, but you can't be fully emotionally present to foster the bond between you and your baby or aid in your child's development if you're not well yourself.

And if you need help in order to make that happen, it's okay to ask for it.

Don't try to delude yourself into being the supermom that society or other seemingly perfect moms have pressured us into being.

There's no such thing as a supermom.

It's all a facade.

Nobody is perfect, and no mother is perfect.

If anyone is trying to make you feel that you need to strive for perfection, please know that it's nonsense!

We all strive to do the best we can for our families with the cards we've been dealt.

Stop comparing yourself to other moms or allowing people to compare you with others. Instead, focus on what's best for you and your child's well-being.

We all have and continue to have moments of greatness and moments where we fail.

That's just part of being a parent and a human being.

Learn to accept that and distance yourself from anyone who tries to make you feel otherwise—especially while you're sick and trying to heal.

The added pressure from others, your own guilt, and your self-comparisons are poisonous to your well-being.

You don't need it convoluting your already confused mind. Focus only on the people and things that truly matter.

Including yourself.

That doesn't make you selfish; that makes you responsible. Responsible for your own health and responsible for the well-being of your child.

But before you can fulfill your role as a mother in its fullest and best form, you need to focus on the responsibility of getting yourself healthy first.

ooooo

I was experiencing so much anxiety and despair that my mind was continuously conflicted with competing thoughts and fears. It was to the point where basic tasks were difficult to do.

Basic necessities like eating, showering, getting dressed, and brushing my teeth became enormous and daunting tasks to fulfill.

Mustering up the mental capacity, motivation, and will to accomplish any of them became unachievable.

My mind and body now had a very finite level of energy, and that was devoted to keeping my son alive; this meant that everything else fell off the grid and became a low priority.

I was almost unrecognizable to those who knew me.

The determined, ambitious, and motivated go-getter who loved socializing with family and friends, exploring fashion, and continuously working toward achieving her goals became a sort of recluse inside her mind's prison.

Socializing with family and friends, laughing, and having fun was replaced with endless tears, conversations about anxiety, despair, self-pity, anger, and fear.

The girl who had always loved fashion and dressing up, who'd never gone a day without doing her hair and makeup—even during university exam seasons—was replaced with an unrecognizable person.

She became a girl who woke up and barely had the energy to wash her face or brush her teeth, and to be honest, some days she just didn't—no, couldn't.

She was replaced with a girl who wore the same dirty shirt and sweatpants or tights day in and day out.

She was replaced with a girl who barely brushed her hair, no longer coloured her grey roots, and pulled it all up in a bun because having the energy to do anything else was out of the question.

Her conversations, once filled with laughter and humour, were replaced with endless tears and discussions about sorrow, despair, and hopelessness.

You get the picture.

She became unrecognizable because that's not who she was.

That's not the person she or those around her knew.

I started to search the internet for articles, books, message boards, and anything that could help me make sense of it all.

I looked for people with similar stories, experiences, or symptoms.

What were they experiencing?

How did they get better?

What other therapies are out there?

Cognitive behavioural therapy, natural and herbal remedies, hypnosis—you name it; I obsessively read about and tried it.

But you see, the problem with scouring the internet and reading too much is that it starts to mess with your head. You start to ruminate about the negative stories and experiences that you read, and it all starts to cloud your already-confused mind and judgement.

I'm not saying educating yourself isn't helpful, but overly obsessing isn't the right approach either.

You see, the problem was, I was so entangled in trying to find someone or something out there to tell me that I wasn't going crazy that I actually started to lose control of my mind even more, and I created an even greater sense of panic within myself. I became trapped in a vicious cycle of overanalyzing and increasing fear, almost like a snowball effect. The more I read about the experiences of others; which were often not the same as mine, the more I panicked.

I became so obsessed with analyzing how I felt and finding treatment that it consumed me and actually led me to sink deeper and deeper into depression and anxiety.

Then one day, a postpartum support worker came to see me. Her name was Cheryl Childs, and she worked at a local non-profit organization.

Cheryl was a beacon of light.

Cheryl is one of the people who saved me.

You see, she'd become a support worker in the area of perinatal mental health because she herself had experienced postpartum mental illness.

She knew everything I was going through and how I was feeling.

Cheryl could not only understand me, but she did so *fully* because she could also relate.

Not to say that my support system of family and close friends didn't understand.

They understood as best as they could. But they couldn't fully relate.

Their understanding was different.

I will elaborate a lot more on this in upcoming chapters where I discuss the role of supporters and how they can truly help you.

Within what must have been less than twenty minutes of speaking to me, Cheryl knew I needed much more intense help.

Right there from my living room, she made the call to the Women's Mental Health Clinic in our city, Calgary.

A clinic with psychiatrists specializing in perinatal mental health.

A clinic that nobody around me seemed to know about.

A clinic that I wish I had been referred to at the onset of my illness.

Nonetheless, Cheryl made the call and explained that I was in dire need of help and needed to be seen as soon as possible.

That day, Cheryl looked me in the eyes and told me that I would get better.

Would, because she had been through it, and she knew how I felt.

That was probably the first time I actually felt there may be hope.

Maybe I would survive this and possibly be myself again.

Thank you, Cheryl.

∞∞∞

My family doctor sent a referral to the Women's Mental Health Clinic, and I was finally set up with an appointment to see Dr. Zahra Mohamed.

The doctor that I attribute to saving me.

To be honest, there are many moments during my journey I don't fully recall in specific detail.

However, I do remember certain points very vividly.

I remember that my first appointment (and let's be honest, subsequent appointments) with Dr. Mohamed was filled with my inability to speak clearly because of an outpouring of unstoppable tears.

I remember thinking, *How do I even begin explaining to her what is happening to me and what's going on in my head?*

But she helped me through it with a combination of being patient, understanding, stern, and humorous all at the same time.

She patiently listened to me as I described what was happening and what my symptoms were.

She helped me understand what the illness itself entailed and what the necessary steps to getting better were.

Sometimes, she needed to be stern, telling me to stop trying to doctor myself, and trust that she was the professional and knew what she was doing.

She also won my trust by getting to know who I was prior to becoming sick.

She asked me what I used to love doing and inquired about the things that used to make me feel happy in order to help me understand that I would one day look forward to those moments again and feel the joy I used to.

But more than anything, I felt that she truly understood what I was experiencing because she told me her story.

She told me that she began specializing in perinatal psychiatry because she herself experienced postpartum mental illness with one of her children.

My goodness, I can't explain the immense calming effect and sudden exponential increase in trust that I developed the moment she uttered those words.

She was no longer just a doctor reiterating theoretical knowledge that she'd read in a medical book.

She was another woman who'd actually endured the torturous experience that I was living through.

She knew how it all felt and what I meant when I described my thoughts, feelings, and symptoms.

And to me, that meant that I could trust her and her opinions.

I have to be honest, though; there were plenty of moments in my sessions with Dr. Mohamed when the anxiety and depression took over and my mind couldn't rationalize properly.

There were moments when she provided me with her professional advice, and I blatantly rolled my eyes at her in disagreement—particularly when she told me that I would recover one day.

Even though those were the very words of hope that I wanted to hear.

Somehow, when she stated them, all of me couldn't believe it.

A small part of me did, because as I said, she went through a similar experience, so if anyone truly knew, it was her.

But the ill part of me, the irrational part of my mind, didn't want to believe the words.

I spent many days on the couch in her office crying, sobbing, and damn near hyperventilating as I tried to make sense of it all. I continued to feel frustrated and fell even deeper into despair.

Why wasn't anything working? Why was I not getting better?

She adjusted my medication, and it partially worked, but then other symptoms arose. She adjusted it again, yet it only partially worked, and my symptoms still persisted.

I have to tell you, in retrospect, I feel bad for her.

She was a phenomenal and patient doctor, and I must have been such a perplexing patient; my mind was all over the place, and my stubborn need for control often complicated the situation even more.

To be honest, having a determined and motivated mind can be such a wonderful thing when you want to be a go-getter and achieve all of your life's goals.

But when you're faced with mental illness and that very same mind is out of control, having the need for control becomes a tremendous battle.

It becomes very difficult to relinquish that sense of control, and for individuals like me who need it, mental illness is an absolutely destructive force.

Nonetheless, Dr. Mohamed continued to persevere with me.

She adjusted my medication again, and one day, she said words to me that helped bring a sense of calmness.

At a time when I felt like all hope was gone and no therapy or medication would ever work for me, she explained that an individual's genetic composition could affect how their bodies metabolized and reacted to medications.

Just because a medication was the most commonly prescribed or deemed the most effective against a particular illness like postpartum depression, it wouldn't necessarily work on all individuals.

Varying ethnicities and genetic compositions could cause their bodies to react differently to medication and could contribute to how an individual's body metabolized the medication.

So, she reassured me that while the first, second, third, and even fourth may not have worked, one eventually would.

As someone who loves learning about human physiology and psychology, those words were music to my ears.

It all logically made sense to me and put the experience into perspective.

I had a much easier time understanding that I shouldn't try to adjust my medications myself or try other remedies that I had read about on the internet without consulting my physician first.

I needed to trust her medical advice and learn that when we found the right combination, I would see progress.

That went a long way in helping me become more patient with the process of finding the right medication (although to be honest, I still wasn't fully patient or compliant).

There were still times when I tried to doctor myself.

Bad idea. Don't do it.

I have to mention that it's also important to find a psychiatrist (or psychologist, counsellor, or therapist) that you have good rapport with.

One that helps you feel at ease.

Because you need the ability to feel comfortable and truly be honest with that individual in order to receive the most beneficial treatment.

If you can't trust the person and fully disclose the truth to them, then you are doing yourself a disservice.

Remember when I said that there are many moments from my illness that I can't recall, but some that I remember vividly?

Well, there was another conversation with Dr. Mohamed that I will never forget.

She gave me the most significant piece of advice, one that helped to remove a mountainous burden of guilt off of my shoulders.

This advice would change me and ultimately contribute toward helping me win my battle against postpartum mental illness.

I now want to share that very same advice with you so that you may use it as an armour of strength to help you or your loved one during the same battle toward recovery.

The conversation took place during one of my typical anguished and tear-filled sessions with her; I vividly recall having a difficult time breathing and trying to speak while attempting to articulate one of my biggest fears:

The fear of the outcome of not feeling the bond and love for my child.

You see, I constantly verbalized that I didn't *feel* love toward him.

Somewhere inside, whether it was my heart or my logical mind, I *knew* that I loved him.

I must.

He's my child.

But as I mentioned before, my mind and heart would not connect.

That day, I remember feeling the most soul-crushing sadness and guilt I'd ever felt in my life.

Crying the hardest and most emotional tears I have ever shed, I asked her, "Dr. Mohamed, tell me—what's going to happen to my son when he grows up and learns that his mom doesn't feel love toward him? What kind of human being will he turn out to be?"

I was so afraid.

So afraid of ruining this little human's life.

Petrified of turning him into a horrible, uncaring person devoid of love, all because I couldn't feel our bond and connection.

You know what she said to me?

I have to tell you, I'm sobbing right now as I even write this.

I can't stop the tears because her answer was so profound.

She asked me, "Yalda, when Amir is hungry, do you feed him?"

I responded, "Well, yeah, of course I do."

She then asked, "When he soils himself, do you change his diaper?"

Again, I answered, "Yes, I do."

She continued, "When he's sleepy, do you put him to sleep? When he's upset and crying, do you pick him up and console him?"

I answered, "Yes."

Then she said it, the most freeing words: "Well, then, you do love him." She explained that babies may interpret and feel love differently than you and I do as adults. To a baby, love means meeting their basic needs for hunger, cleanliness, sleep, and comfort.

As adults, our interpretation of love is filled with a multitude of experiences, feelings, and thought processes that lead us to determine whether or not we feel loved.

But to a baby, meeting those basic needs helps them feel the bond and connection of love.

In that moment I felt reassured that Amir did feel loved by me because I was one of the individuals taking care of him. I fed him when he was hungry, changed him when he soiled himself, picked up and consoled him when he cried, and put him to sleep when he was tired.

"So he's going to turn out just fine, because to him, he feels loved," she said.

Her words felt like water being poured over a hot flame.

So much of the shame, guilt, and worry I had felt up to that point dissipated from within me.

Now I could concentrate on getting better, and the fear of destroying this child's life was drastically lessened with those simple words.

So, I say this to you, any mother feeling the immense guilt of wondering whether you love your baby, love them enough, don't love them right away, or love them but don't feel the connection or bond yet: know that you are loving them!

Because a baby's interpretation of love is different than ours as adults.

So, trust that once you overcome this illness and feel like yourself again, that emotional bond and connection will present itself in its entirety and truest form.

Once your mind calms down and lets you rationalize and feel again, you will see that you have always loved your child—right from the start.

Then you will also *feel* it with all of your heart and soul, just as I did.

∞∞∞∞

Although I had that very profound conversation with Dr. Mohamed, my mind was still severely ill. I continued to experience anxiety and depression. But I also started developing a new set of rather strange symptoms and thoughts as well.

I began doubting reality and the world around me.

I felt like I was in a strange dream.

Everything around me looked and seemed normal, but it didn't *feel* normal.

I started to doubt whether I was truly experiencing the day-to-day moments of my life or if it was all a strange dream. I had a hard time deciphering between reality and this potential dream state.

I started to doubt whether my son was actually real.

I kept saying, "I know he's real and he exists, but why doesn't he feel real? I know he's my son; I know I gave birth to him. I know that I'm supposed to love him, but I can't feel it, and it all doesn't seem real."

I went as far as starting to pinch my own skin and that of others around me to see if people were real or whether they were a part of my dream world and a figment of my imagination.

I would stare at those around me in a strange, empty, and emotion-less way.

I often "spaced out," as my friends and family referred to it.

My eyes looked blank.

I was experiencing what are known as delusions and symptoms of depersonalization that are often associated with really severe depression and even psychosis.

I was prescribed antipsychotic medication for these new symptoms, and again, the saga of finding the right type and dosage of medication continued.

I won't bore you with all of the details, but this went on for a while, and as my symptoms kept progressing, Dr. Mohamed continuously kept asking me if I ever felt or had thoughts of harming myself or others.

To which I answered, "No."

She kept reminding me that if I ever reached the point where I felt that I needed immediate help, I should go to the hospital, and it was okay for me to do so.

You see, I was afraid of ever getting to the point where I would need to be hospitalized in a psychiatric ward.

Why?

Because in my mind, it would mean that I had officially become crazy.

And once that happened, I would clearly be deemed an unfit mother, and my child would be taken away from me forever.

I was petrified of those thoughts.

Eventually, December rolled around, and by this point, Amir was nearly six months old.

However, I was still quite unwell and not improving the way I was hoping to.

My family decided that we should take a trip to Mexico together in the hopes that taking some time away from it all, away from the everyday routine and responsibilities of life, would help me destress and potentially ease my mind.

That's what we all thought and hoped for.

By now, I'm sure you've realized that nothing ever seemed to go the way I hoped.

I spent nearly every waking moment of that entire week in Mexico crying.

Whether it was the first thing in the morning, during breakfast, at the poolside, at dinner, during the entertainment shows, you name it—at some point or another, I cried and was consumed with anxiety.

My poor family—they tried so hard to help me and continued to be patient.

To this day, I can't thank them enough for their love and patience during my illness.

They endured it all alongside me, and they were the glue that held me together.

Remember when I mentioned that Dr. Mohamed kept asking me if I had ever thought of harming myself or others?

Well, by the time Mexico came around, that changed.

At this point, the misery of it all had become so unbearable that I constantly wished I would die and that it would all end.

In fact, I prayed for it all the time.

I begged God to take me every single day.

I was never going to take my own life, but boy did I wish for God to do so.

Apparently, God had other plans (very thankfully so).

I'll never forget one particular day in Mexico.

We were all at the poolside, and my husband had organized a massage appointment for me close by.

Again, in the hopes that the relaxation would help to ease my mind and destress me.

I remember lying on the massage table, and partway during the treatment, out of nowhere, with a complete lack of forewarning, I suddenly had a thought pop into my mind.

You need to kill your son.

I don't know if I'm capable of adequately explaining what that moment truly felt like.

It was a combination of the most horrific, fear-inducing experience imaginable, a feeling of my heart beating out of my chest, and an inability to breathe as I gasped for air, trying to process and make sense of what had just gone through my mind.

My head felt as though it had sent my mind into a spinning whirlwind of competing thoughts, waiting to explode.

I remember the gut-wrenching and nauseating sadness that consumed me as my eyes quickly filled with tears and my entire body shook in fear.

I recall telling the massage therapist to stop, quickly putting my clothes on, and running toward my mom, who was at the poolside, tending to Amir while the rest of my family was in the water.

I was in a complete state of panic with my eyes so full of tears, I could barely see the path clearly.

I could hardly speak through my tears and short breaths as I sobbed inconsolably and tried to explain what I had just experienced.

Trying to conjure up the words to explain that my mind had just told me I needed to take my son's life.

How?

How could I think that?

How could any mother think that?

Why could I think that?

My mom kept telling me over and over again, "It's okay. It's just a bad thought. You're not harming anyone. He's safe. You haven't hurt him. You're going to be okay. It's just a bad thought. Breathe. Calm down and try to breathe. You're going to be all right; this is just the depression talking."

At this point, my husband and sisters had all come out of the water, and it became the family's mission to console and calm me down.

I can't tell you how much I love and adore my family, because in that moment, they all saved me—as they had done for the past six months.

Soon after, our Mexico trip came to an end, and we returned back home.

I felt some relief in knowing that the harmful thought had not returned for the remainder of the trip.

However, I was still quite ill, and all of my symptoms remained—including my delusions about reality.

ooooo

It was shortly after we returned from Mexico that I experienced the most pivotal, life-altering moment of my illness.

This was one of those vividly remembered moments.

A day that I will never forget for as long as I live.

A day that I can't get out of my mind, and the day that completely changed my life.

I was at my mom's house, sitting on her carpet as I changed Amir's diaper on his changing pad.

I got up to throw away the diaper. He just laid there, this beautiful, smiling little boy looking up at me, and as I stood up, it happened again.

It came back.

The thought to kill him.

The thought said, *You need to kill him.*

Except this time, involuntarily, unconsciously, and unwillingly, as I held on to the diaper and looked at him, I raised my leg up to crush his skull with my foot.

I don't know how that moment happened so quickly. I just remember my foot being raised, hovering above his head, and before I lowered it, somehow, whether it was God or my conscious mind, I suddenly snapped out of it and realized what I was about to do.

I remember the fear that consumed me as I came to the realization of what I had almost done. I immediately dropped the diaper and moved away from my son.

I screamed with every ounce of my being for my mom to come and help.

I don't think I had ever screamed so loudly before in my life.

I remember my poor mom; her eyes were filled with fear as she rushed to the room to come to my rescue.

"Take him from me. I'm going to hurt him. Take him—I can't be around him. I need to go to the hospital." I recall repeating those words as my entire body trembled in fear.

I asked her to call my husband to come and take me to the hospital.

That was the defining moment for me.

The moment when my biggest fears came true.

The moment when I realized that I wasn't improving and could truly come close to harming Amir.

It was the moment when my fears of being hospitalized and having my son taken away from me were overcome with the fear of being a mom who killed her child.

It was the moment when selfishness had to be replaced with selflessness.

The moment when the repercussions of the *what ifs* and *what coulds* pertaining to myself had to be replaced with doing whatever it took to ensure my child's safety and well-being.

The moment when it no longer mattered if he was taken from me and I never saw him again; at least I could ensure that he would live and I would not be the one to take his life.

It's hard to explain that moment.

Because to you, reader, it may seem ridiculous that in the three seconds it takes an individual to stand up, their mind can take them from a normal standing position to unknowingly lifting their leg to inflict such an unfathomable fate onto their baby and then suddenly snapping out of it before possibly ending a life.

How can all of that happen in such a small timeframe?

It's hard to explain the how, but I promise you, it's possible, and knowing that is horrifying.

What's even more horrifying is knowing that I am not the only mother who has ever experienced the unspeakable.

Yet so many fear speaking up and asking for help.

This is why I wrote this book and why I share my story.

Because I was not, nor will I ever be, the only one.

I hope that this book will help anyone who comes even close to this scenario.

I want to ensure that the next mother who has the unimaginable thought of harming themselves or their child the *first* time has the strength, courage, and support to seek help *immediately!*

To be honest, it wasn't only the thought of harming my son that scared me.

But the realization, and in a sense, validation, that at this point I was truly losing my mind, and myself, to such an extensive degree that I needed to be hospitalized.

The realization that as a human being, as a mother, I'd had the thought of taking a life.

The life of my own child.

And I had lost so much control of my mind and body that without intending to do so, I had somehow managed to physically come close to accomplishing the unthinkable.

I can't truly explain to you what that knowledge feels like.

To know that your mind, a part of you, wanted you to take the life of someone so dear to you.

Someone who, by all rights, is your entire world.

It's a really difficult concept to come to terms with and accept.

I won't lie; for a long time, I dealt with a lot of guilt and sadness associated with it.

I let the guilt eat away at me.

But I didn't need to feel that guilt.

Having those thoughts wasn't my fault.

I didn't *choose* to have them or to become ill.

That wasn't me.

That person, that mind, those thoughts, those weren't *me*.

They weren't Yalda.

They didn't represent who I truly am.

The Yalda I know would never inflict harm upon anyone, let alone her child, her greatest source of love.

Please, if you or your loved one have come remotely close to experiencing any of the things I've mentioned, or if your depressed and anxious mind has taken over so much that you can no longer recognize yourself or control your thoughts or actions, *get help now!*

I beg of you, don't wait. Please, get help.

Don't be afraid.

I know there is the fear of the unknown.

The fear of being hospitalized and being given a mental illness label, the uncertainty of what will happen to your child, and whether or not you will ever be able to see them again.

But don't let that fear consume you.

Don't let that fear overcome your judgement and interfere with seeking help.

You, or your loved one, are ill.

There is nothing to be ashamed of in knowing that.

You didn't choose to become ill.

However, you do have the choice to stop it from worsening.

You do have the choice to take the steps necessary to overcome this illness and be healthy again.

You do have the choice to keep your child and yourself free from harm.

So please, make the right choice and speak up if you've ever experienced what I've described.

∞∞∞

Poor Kaveh.

I can only imagine how he felt and what went through his mind when he arrived at my mom's house and heard what had happened.

Not only did my biggest fear come to fruition that day, but so did his.

Yet it had to happen.

I had to be hospitalized, and we both knew it.

And so, we went.

We left Amir with my mom, and Kaveh took me to the emergency department of the hospital.

I don't remember her name or what she looked like, but I remember the triage nurse who spoke to me.

I remember sitting in the chair, my eyes streaming with tears of anguish as I recollected the events of that day to her.

I recall telling her that I didn't care if they needed to take my son away from me; I didn't want to harm him.

With the most agonizing sadness, I told her, "I don't want to be the mom that kills him. Please, just help me. Take me away from him. I need help."

God bless her.

I remember she leaned over, held my hands, looked me in the eyes, and said, "Nobody is going to take your son away from you. But right now, you are very, very sick and need help." Then she said, "I want to thank you for coming to the hospital and getting help. I know how hard that was to do. But do you know how many mothers are afraid of asking for help, and they suffer in silence? Or even worse, end up harming themselves or their child because of that fear? Thank you for realizing you need help and coming here today."

Reassurance.

That's all I needed.

Reassurance in knowing that I was going to get the help I needed and that my son wasn't going to be taken away.

That's all I needed to move forward and heal.

I signed documents stating that although I voluntarily checked myself into the hospital, I was no longer voluntarily allowed to leave until a doctor deemed me medically fit to do so.

I'm mentioning all of this because I think it's important to be educated and knowledgeable about what to expect.

I know it can be scary to think that you may have to relinquish control to someone else—to doctors.

But when you are at the point where your mind can quickly take over and convolute all sense of rationalization, then you do, to an extent, need to relinquish some of that control to medical professionals who can help you regain control of your mind.

And not everyone who gets hospitalized may be expected to relinquish that control, but in instances like mine where the severity of my illness was extreme and the possibility of causing harm to myself or others was high, the need to sign away control was necessary as a life-saving precaution.

For me, the fear of signing away my control was outweighed by the fear of what could happen if I didn't get the help I needed.

So I had to trust the process and believe that temporarily relinquishing that control was worth it in the long run.

∞∞∞

I spent three weeks in the psychiatric ward of the hospital; initially, I was under strict suicide watch protocols where I was not able to leave the unit at all.

My son was also not allowed onto the unit, and very rightfully so, because it would have jeopardized his safety.

Therefore, he remained under the care of my husband and my mom during my stay at the hospital.

My medications were strongly adjusted, I was constantly monitored, and I met with a psychiatrist on a daily basis.

I remember one day in particular as I sat on the hospital bed, sobbing and praying.

I looked up and said, "God, I know you made me sick for a reason, and I'll be damned if I don't find out why. Please help me and give me the strength to overcome this so that one day, I can understand why I became ill and why, out of all the people I know, you chose me to endure this hardship."

This moment is why.

This book is why.

Loving my son the way I do and having the bond that I now have with him is why.

Being able to help others facing the same horrific experience is why.

Raising awareness and being a voice for those who are too afraid to speak up is why.

There are so many *whys*, and I will elaborate on more of them in a later chapter, but for now, rest assured that I know why I became ill. Believe it or not, I'm grateful for the experience.

As I improved, my husband was also allowed to take me off of the unit and let me see our son for small increments of time each day.

The first time was for ten minutes, then fifteen, then twenty. Soon I got to spend an hour outside of the ward with my family.

My family—especially my husband—knew how instrumental seeing Amir was for my ability to heal.

They knew how important it was for Amir's development to have that bond with his mom.

As well as how important it was for me to develop that bond with him.

My husband fought for me.

According to him, he told the doctor, "I know my wife. My wife is a caring, loving, and compassionate person. My wife loves our son, even though right now, she doesn't think or feel it. She needs to see him and to bond with him in order to heal. Not allowing her to see him will crush her and only make her get worse. She needs this child to help her heal. He is the reason she will get better. Trust me, I know my wife."

He was right.

I continued to slowly improve with each passing day until I was finally at a point where it was safe again for me to be released from the hospital.

Don't get me wrong, I wasn't back to my normal self quite yet.

I still had symptoms of anxiety and depression, but the severity of the symptoms was lowered to a point where I could be under the supervision of my own psychiatrist and doctor, and I no longer had to be under hospital protection.

I need to take a minute to also explain how invaluable others' support was during my time at the hospital.

The support of my family, who continuously reminded me that I was loved and that I could rely on them to make it through the battle.

My husband and mom, who shifted their work and daily responsibilities to take care of Amir while I was hospitalized, and my sisters, who constantly reassured me that I wasn't alone.

The support of friends who took the time to visit me and give me a sense of hope.

The support of my husband's managers and co-workers who allowed him the ability to alter his work schedule and deliverables in order to take care of Amir while I was away.

I mention all of this because the psychiatric ward of a hospital is not a fun place to be.

It can even seem scary at times.

But let me tell you, it's much less scary than the thought of harming your child or taking a life.

It's a place where you can feel safe in knowing that you will get help.

It's a place where you can feel safe in knowing that you are provided around-the-clock monitoring and are seen by professionals who specialize in mental health—professionals who are knowledgeable in providing you with the treatment you need.

However, the thing that can give you the strength and courage to overcome the fear of being hospitalized is having the support of those around you.

Having people who remind you that you are loved, cared for, and give you a sense of hope and reassurance goes a tremendous way in helping you heal.

Even if there's only one person who is showing you love and support, that's all you need to feel a boost in strength and courage.

Take a moment to ask yourself this: Am I, or is my loved one, in a situation where the symptoms are so severe that hospitalization should be considered?

Be honest with yourself.

Trying to come up with justifications to convince or fool yourself that hospitalization isn't necessary won't help you or your loved one going through this experience.

If being hospitalized is required, don't be afraid.

Because for some of us, it may be the necessary and life-saving option.

And that is okay.

For me, having the self-awareness that I needed to be hospitalized and taking the steps to do so was the best decision I ever made.

It saved my life and the life of my son, which made the entire experience a worthy life lesson.

∞∞∞

It took me another two years after being released from the hospital to finally be me again.

The recovery process was long and slow, but it was just that: recovery.

After my hospitalization, I was finally in a place where I had the right medications, support system, strength, and motivation to keep fighting the battle.

There were good days and bad days.

Days filled with positivity and hope and days filled with a sense of failure and sadness.

But through it all, there was gradual and constant improvement.

Through it all, there was support for me to keep going.

I slowly regained my sense of self.

I slowly regained my ability to think, feel, and love again.

By January 2016, I was well enough that I was able to stop taking antipsychotic medication.

This was a huge milestone for me. It meant that my delusions and confusion about reality had ceased.

And this was definitely something to celebrate.

I continued to take an antidepressant medication, but by this point, my dosage had gone from the highest possible to the lowest. But to help diminish my chances of a relapse, my doctor and I agreed to keep me on the medication for a while longer.

Finally, in August 2016 as we celebrated my sister Ayda's wedding, I got to a place where I no longer needed any medication at all.

I was free from postpartum mental illness.

I've been grateful for the experience and every moment since, full of gratitude and love for my son, and ready to live my new life.

So, where am I now?

You'll find out in the final chapter.

In the meantime, for those of you who may not know first-hand, let me take you on a deeper journey in trying to help you understand what it actually feels like to have symptoms of anxiety, depression, and psychosis.

2
HOW IT FELT

What do the symptoms of depression, anxiety, or psychosis really feel like? Many of us are aware of the symptoms as stated in the multitudes of textbooks, medical journals, articles, and websites.

But do you really know what they feel like?

Let me tell you, unless you have actually experienced them first-hand, you don't truly know.

Now, I don't claim to be a magician who can miraculously let you feel the actual feelings associated with these ailments.

But I'm hoping to get you as close to understanding them as I possibly can.

Why?

Because in the event that you're experiencing them, you'll know that you're not alone despite your mind telling you otherwise.

And if you're surrounded by or supporting someone who is experiencing them, then maybe this will allow you to have a better, more helpful, and empathetic understanding of what they're going through.

The occurrence of anxious or depressive thoughts and feelings are not necessarily unique to each person.

They often occur in similar ways to others experiencing these ailments, and the underlying foundation is quite similar as well.

Let me be clear: this is not to say that you are not unique and your experience is not unique.

That is absolutely not the case.

You and your experience are entirely unique.

For each of us, our life experiences, current life circumstances, support systems, resources, and knowledge bases play a tremendous role in how our experience with depression and anxiety unfolds.

However, the gut-wrenching sadness, hopelessness, loneliness, lack of motivation, inability to concentrate or think, and nauseating sense of fear or danger are common and not unique.

Guess what?

That revelation is actually a really good thing.

Do you know why?

Because it means that what works for one may work for another.

Our combined experiences with mental illness have taught us lessons and strategies to overcome symptoms, and you can use others' experiences to help you or your loved ones heal as well.

It means there is hope, and you are not alone.

I have to be honest, though; I don't know if I can truly help you understand what symptoms of psychosis feel like.

That one is tough. That one is scary, and it's not for the faint of heart.

I don't know if I can adequately do it justice.

But I can try to explain my own experience with it and what it entailed in hopes that you can appreciate the severity and imminent danger associated with it and why it's so critical to seek medical help immediately.

ooooo

Let's begin with anxiety.

We've all heard the phrases *feeling anxious* or *experiencing anxiety* thrown out there.

But do you really know what anxiety feels like?

Do you know what the experience actually entails?

I'm going to try and walk you through it.

I want you to imagine getting on a roller coaster.

Now, for some of you, this may be a fun and exhilarating thought. If so, try to imagine something that is a lot less pleasant for you.

But for those of you who aren't necessarily thrill seekers, imagine you are now riding this roller coaster, and it's approaching the uphill climb to the highest and steepest peak.

Imagine your heart racing in anticipation of knowing that the car is climbing closer and closer to the top, and once it gets there, it's going to plummet downhill as fast as it can go.

How do you feel?

Are you clenching your hands, pursing your lips, breathing harder?

Is your heart starting to race a bit, your stomach starting to feel a little queasy?

Is your body feeling shaky?

Are you increasingly feeling worried in anticipation of this steep fall?

Are you suddenly wanting to run away, escape the confines of the seat, and just get to neutral ground where you can avoid the dip?

Now you know how someone with anxiety feels when they are trying to avoid situations.

These can be public or social situations, or they can be fears of something bad happening to them or their loved ones. In my case, I feared being alone with my child and going to sleep every night.

People with anxiety continuously experience intrusive thoughts, fears, and worries that keep amplifying as they ruminate about them over and over again. They want to stop thinking about it all, but they can't, and it consumes them.

Now that you've felt what the anticipation feels like, let me try to explain the experience of being fully immersed in anxiousness and the resulting feelings and emotions.

Get back on that roller coaster.

Except now, oh, you're at the top.

There's no going back.

You're about to plummet down that ride as fast as it can take you.

Ready . . . ? Drop!

How do you feel?

Do your eyes feel as though they're about to pop out of their sockets from fear?

Is your heart racing so quickly that you feel as though it's about to explode out of your chest?

Does your head feel heavy and hurt?

Are your limbs shaking?

Can you speak up and verbalize your fear when you're short of breath?

And the worst feeling of all . . . does your stomach feel like it's in knots and churning to the point that you feel you're about to vomit?

Does it feel as though death could be imminent at any moment?

That's probably the best way I can describe full-blown anxiety.

Like the drop of a roller coaster.

Except that you're not lucky enough to have it end in less than ten seconds like an actual roller-coaster drop.

Oh, no, it can last all day long.

You're clenching your teeth together, and your jaw aches as you try to avoid feeling the fear and panic while your stomach is turning.

Now, be honest with yourself.

Imagine you experienced that roller-coaster drop, all day, every day.

Do you think you could function?

Do you think you could concentrate and focus?

Could you perform at work the way you used to?

Could you go about your daily routine, completing your tasks and responsibilities as you used to?

Could you maintain relationships like you did previously?

Could you take care of yourself?

Could you think about consuming food, showering, getting dressed, tidying up your home, visiting with friends and family, going out to the movies, or going to the gym?

More importantly, could you take care of a newborn baby when you felt that way?

Do you now understand why it's so hard for a person dealing with anxiety to function or act "normal" in their day-to-day interactions?

Do you now understand why it's important to show them support and compassion and help them through the process?

Because believe me, none of us like being on that continuous roller-coaster drop day in and day out.

None of us like feeling that panic and fear every moment of the day as we try to accomplish basic tasks.

Do you now understand why it's so hard for someone to do everything they used to do when they're experiencing anxiety?

Because when it hits, and when it takes over, it consumes you entirely.

For those of you experiencing anxiety, you must slowly teach yourself how to stop it from consuming you.

How to accomplish daily tasks while that feeling is present.

Because once you learn how to do that, the anxiety starts to slowly diminish, and it will have less control over your mind.

Once you accept that it's a part of your day, it won't be able to consume you the way it does when you try to resist it.

ooooo

Did you enjoy that roller-coaster analogy?

I'm going to venture a guess and say probably not.

Do you now want to know what being depressed feels like?

Well, I'm going to tell you anyway.

Imagine yourself at the happiest moment in your life.

A moment when you felt utterly confident in yourself and your abilities.

A moment when you've accomplished an important life or career goal and are feeling on top of the world.

When you're looking and feeling your best.

Your days and nights are filled with love, happiness, laughter, family, friends, hobbies, vacations, good food, and the opportunities are endless.

A moment when you felt that you could take on the world.

Now, this perfect day couldn't get any better, so rest your head on your pillow and wait as the next blissful day arrives.

I'm sorry, but it appears that you haven't woken up to bliss.

You've actually woken up feeling empty.

You can't quite put your finger on it, but you don't feel like yourself.

You're overwhelmed with this unexplainable sadness that takes a hold of your soul, and you don't know how to shake it.

This feeling of loneliness that leaves you feeling helpless even when you're surrounded by others and are, by definition, not alone at all.

Even when you're supported by others.

A feeling where you can't think like you used to.

You no longer seem to have that drive and motivation to reach your aspirations or goals.

Heck, you don't really have *any* aspirations or goals anymore.

Your ability to care about things has dissipated.

Pause for a minute here.

Let me clarify that depression itself doesn't have a sudden onset; my description is just to show how depression feels.

It's actually a progressively worsening experience where your mind's focus and consumption of negative thoughts and feelings increase more and more each day as you sink deeper and deeper into the illness.

But for the purpose of helping you conceptualize the experience, I'm describing it in a quick and sudden format.

Please be cognizant of that as you continue reading.

You're now having a really hard time moving out of bed.

The alarm has gone off, but your eyes just don't want to open.

Your body doesn't want to pull the sheets back and get out.

What's happening?

You finally gather the strength and awareness to get yourself out of bed.

You go to the bathroom and wash your face.

Except when you look at yourself in the mirror, you don't really recognize the person looking back.

Your eyes look different.

Lifeless and empty.

That sparkle and joy they once possessed isn't there.

Your hair is a mess.

Your breath smells bad.

Your eyebrows are bushy and unkempt.

Your lips and skin look cracked and dry.

You definitely need a shower.

You think to yourself, *Why do I look so grim? I should clean myself up.*

Except somehow, you can't.

You want to, but you can't.

The thought of picking up that toothbrush, putting toothpaste on it, placing it in your mouth, brushing for two minutes, and then spitting and rinsing seems daunting and difficult.

Forget even caring about your hair, skin, makeup, or clothes.

Are you kidding me?

Who cares what your hair looks like?

The most you can do is pull it back or brush it (on a good day).

Makeup and skincare?

What!

Your brain doesn't even think of those things.

It can't.

Getting dressed?

Pick the first thing you find in your closet or on the floor.

But didn't you wear that yesterday and the day before?

Hmmm, did you?

You can't really remember.

Who cares? It doesn't matter.

Just put it on.

Let's try to make it through the day.

What happened there?

Getting dressed in the morning used to bring you joy and excitement.

You loved looking polished and put together.

But why don't you care anymore?

That's weird.

It's not like you.

Did you forget to shower?

To be honest, the thought of that extra step is too hard to handle.

Taking your clothes off, getting into the shower, washing your hair, washing your body, possibly shaving, coming out of the shower, and then drying your hair?

That would consume way too much brain power and effort.

You can't even think of that many steps.

It's not happening today.

Suddenly, you feel an overwhelming force come over you.

An instant sadness and fear, and all you can do is sit on the bathroom floor and cry.

You cry because you don't recognize yourself.

Both physically and mentally.

You sob because you don't know what's happening to you.

But you recognize that you're slowly slipping away.

The person you knew doesn't seem to be there anymore.

You finally stop feeling sorry for yourself, pick yourself up off the floor, and go downstairs.

You're going to make it through the day. That's what you tell yourself.

You should probably eat something, though.

Except the thought of making food and the effort of preparing it seems really difficult.

Just grab the quickest thing you can put in your mouth.

Who cares if it's healthy or not?

But even the simple act of physically putting food in your mouth, chewing, and swallowing is daunting and nauseating.

Every bite feels like you have a giant rock to swallow, and the pit of your stomach feels so full that adding an ounce of food inside makes you want to throw up.

But you force a few bites down anyway.

Now go to work.

Try to focus on your tasks.

Try to reply to emails and phone calls while you feel unmotivated to do so.

Your boss asks you to step into a meeting room for a chat.

It appears you've missed some important deadlines, and you're not performing at the level they have come to expect from you.

You used to care.

You used to work so hard to prove how dedicated, motivated, and competent you were.

But why can't you exert that level of effort now?

Quick.

Run.

Head over to the bathroom before any of your co-workers or your boss sees you.

Shut the lock, sit on the toilet, hold your hands against your mouth so nobody can hear you, and sob.

What's happening to you?

Why can't you get it together?

Why can't you focus?

Why can't you control your emotions?

The smallest gesture or words make you break down and burst into tears.

You can't seem to control your emotions and thoughts anymore.

After a few minutes of crying, you pick yourself up, wipe away the tears, and try to get back out there and pretend you're okay.

After work, you meet with a friend.

You've always loved hanging out with your friends and sharing stories, going shopping, eating delicious food, and just laughing.

You sit across from one another.

They share stories about their day, their latest accomplishments, what their plans are for the weekend, what they plan to do this summer, and so on and so forth.

They order your favourite dish because they know how much you love it.

But all you can do is look at it and stare.

Inside, you really want to be attentive and care about what they're saying to you.

You really want to smile and be happy for them, but you can't.

Your eyes just blankly stare.

Your mind forgets the words your friend uttered three seconds ago.

Somehow, your mouth has forgotten how to smile or laugh.

You can't keep up with the conversation.

You just sit there and nod.

You utter a few random words here and there and put on a fake smile every so often, but there's no way in hell you are actually carrying on a full conversation.

You can barely think of the words to say, let alone articulate them.

Your favourite dish suddenly has no aspect of favouritism anymore. It tastes just like the last meal you consumed.

Jokes that used to make you laugh hysterically are no longer funny.

In the evening, you used to always go to the gym, jog outside, or even walk to the local park and enjoy the scenery.

Now all you want to do is go home, lie down, and stare into space or go to sleep as you think about your day and how all the remaining days of your life are going to be the same.

You're never going to find enjoyment in life or the things you used to do anymore.

It will be the same sad, mundane, lifeless day for the rest of your life, and you're never going to get better.

Don't forget, here's another opportunity for you to feel hopeless and sad and shed tears about your grim future.

What happened to you?

The happy, motivated, ambitious, funny, loving, hard-working individual you knew has disappeared.

You want to laugh, love, be happy, converse with others, socialize, eat delicious food, dress up, dance, go for a jog, land that important client, go on a superb summer vacation, and just plain enjoy life.

But you can't.

Your mind won't let you.

It won't let you think of doing those things.

And when you do have the momentary ability to think about them, it won't let you feel the enjoyment in those thoughts.

When you're doing any of them, your mind won't let you feel the happiness.

All it tells you is that life is hopeless, you are helpless, and you will remain like this forever.

Now you have a rough idea of what it feels like to be severely depressed.

You want to stop it.

You want to do all the things you used to do.

You want to feel, you want to smile, you want to accomplish, you want to care, and you want to think positively, but you just can't.

It doesn't register in your mind.

Sometimes, you force yourself to go out and do the things you used to do, putting on a fake smile and looking put together or posting a nice picture of yourself on social media, but it's all fake; it's just to save face.

Inside, you feel sad, empty, and lost.

You desperately want to control your emotions, but the tears and sadness overwhelm you.

They come out of nowhere and crush any possible glimmer of hope and happiness that may be coming your way.

Can you now understand why it's so hard for a person dealing with anxiety or depression to carry on conversations or do simple tasks?

It's not that they're lazy or incompetent.

It's not that they don't want to or choose not to do these tasks.

They mentally and physically can't because of everything that is taking place internally within their body and mind.

It's not that they don't want to think positively or aren't trying.

Their mind won't let them.

The negative thoughts overpower the positive ones.

Think about it.

What happens when the one organ that controls your entire body, your entire sense of being and sense of self, is the one that's no longer functioning properly?

It's completely out of control.

It feels as though you're a trapped prisoner in your own mind.

You have a very conscious understanding of who you used to be and what you used to be able to accomplish, but you can't seem to let that person back out.

It's not like breaking your arm and fixing it with a simple cast.

It's not like having a headache and being able to take medication to make it go away in an hour.

The part of your body that isn't working is the part that controls everything else.

When it starts malfunctioning, it makes everything else in your body malfunction with it.

Nothing seems to work as it used to.

Not only do you start to experience mood-altering symptoms, but you experience physical malfunctions as well.

You have a hard time sleeping.

You have a hard time waking up.

Your limbs hurt.

Maybe it's because you used to exercise, but you no longer have the drive to do so.

You start to experience more headaches.

Maybe it's because you spend so much time straining your eyes from crying that it puts pressure on your head.

Some lose their appetite, leading to other health concerns.

Some fill the sadness with food and gain weight, again leading to other health concerns.

You're stuck.

You're yearning to get your old self back, but your mind is enclosed in a jail of solid steel, and all you have are your fingers to break through with.

How do you find the ability or strength to break free?

It seems this mental enclosure has no light coming through it.

I'm here to tell you that there is a hole with light at the end of that jail.

For some of you, as was the case with me, the hole may be tiny and more difficult to see through.

For others, you may be lucky. It's wider with a more visible path to the light.

Either way, there *is* a light.

You just have to stay strong, courageous, and determined.

You can never give up hope.

Try as hard as you can, then try even harder than that.

You must constantly remind yourself that you will break free of this and get yourself back.

You must also surround yourself with people who support you and make you feel cared for.

This includes medical professionals, family, and friends.

Don't try to be a hero, alone in this.

In the end, you are still the ultimate hero.

But let others help you reach that victorious milestone.

To supporters, please be there for those suffering with mental illness so they can get off of their mental roller coasters and walk to safer ground.

Be forgiving.

Be patient.

Be kind.

Whether that's to yourself or your loved one.

When we are consumed by anxiety and depression, we can't always think clearly.

We can't rationalize normally.

Things that are said or done may not be commonly expected from our "normal" selves.

But that's exactly it.

During the illness, we are not functioning as our "normal" selves.

Be patient, kind, forgiving, and understanding.

It goes a long way in helping the recovery process.

ooooo

Postpartum psychosis.

As previously mentioned, with a prevalence rate of 0.001–0.002 percent of births, it is often experienced by those with a diagnosed or undiagnosed presence of bipolar disorder.[6]

However, psychosis symptoms can still occur for those with no presence or history of bipolar disorder as well, such as myself. Also, to be clear, I did not fit the standard medical definition of postpartum psychosis; typically, that has an early postpartum onset within the first four weeks.

I was diagnosed with a major depressive episode with psychosis with postpartum onset and a Not Otherwise Specified (NOS) anxiety disorder with postpartum onset. Basically, these diagnoses implied that my depression, anxiety, and later-developing symptoms of psychosis were initiated postpartum, but at varying times following the birth of my son.

So, how do I define the most horrific experience of my life in words that will make sense or make you even come close to understanding how it felt?

A nightmare.

It's like being in a nightmare that you can't wake up from.

It's like being in a different world.

A dark and empty world.

A world that only you seem to be a part of.

A world where logic doesn't exist.

A world deprived of emotions, feelings, and empathy.

A world where unimaginable thoughts come to mind, and sometimes, actions follow suit.

A world where you question your own existence and the existence of others.

Where every aspect of your being is in question.

It's a world where you can't distinguish between reality and your fictitious mind.

A world where you question everything.

A place where you feel petrified that you will never recover and be the person you knew again.

A place where you feel completely vulnerable. It's as though your mind has betrayed you, and you can no longer trust it or yourself.

Imagine not being able to distinguish whether everything and everyone you have ever known is real.

You constantly question experiences and whether they actually occurred or not.

You question your thoughts and whether they're really your own.

Sometimes, they're very dark thoughts that uncontrollably arise in your mind.

A lot of us have grown up hearing stories on the news of mothers who have killed their children, abandoned their babies in dumpsters, or other unimaginably monstrous acts.

How many of you have heard of these types of stories and thought to yourselves, *What kind of horrible and heartless monster would do that to her own child? What kind of murderous psychopath is she?*

It's okay.

I'm not judging you, and you shouldn't judge yourself either.

I used to think the very same thing.

Until the *thing* happened to me, and I became that mother.

It wasn't until I experienced this horrific illness that I came to understand what a lot of those women endured.

None of us want to come close to being a mother who wishes harm upon her child.

In fact, most of us are perfectly normal and functioning members of society.

We are hard workers, individuals who love, care deeply, and are filled with compassion.

But then suddenly, something is triggered within us.

We give birth to a baby, and we lose control of our minds and all sense of logic.

Without any desire to do so.

As a mother, the thought of harm coming to your child is one of the most fear-inducing concepts.

Just imagine the thought of being the one to cause that harm.

Psychosis feels like you have relinquished control of your mind. It no longer seems to connect with your body, consciousness, or rationality.

It's a feeling of entrapment.

It's a feeling of being controlled by an external force.

A force that no longer lets you distinguish between right and wrong.

It's hard to explain what it feels like, living with that knowledge.

Living with the fact that I could have ended my son's life.

It hurts my heart.

Once, it ate away at my soul.

It's something that will never leave me.

But I no longer feel any guilt or shame because of it.

Why?

Because although I can't take back the thoughts that occurred or the experiences that happened, I can feel damn proud of the fact that even in that state of mind, I recognized that something was wrong and sought help.

I asked for help before it became detrimental.

I refuse to feel guilty and ashamed, because *I didn't choose to become ill*, and neither has any other mother who has experienced, or will experience, postpartum mental illness or psychosis symptoms.

The only choice that I did make was to admit to myself and my support system that I was not well and needed help.

The choice I did make was to be courageous and strong in order to fight for my life and my son's.

You can do so as well.

Postpartum psychosis is considered a medical emergency.

It's not an illness to take lightly.

If you're experiencing any delusions, hallucinations, or thoughts that don't make sense, immediately seek medical attention.

This illness is not something to joke around with, but it is treatable.

That part, you *can* choose.

Seek help before it's too late.

ooooo

By now, you have a slightly more defined sense of what anxiety, depression, and psychosis feel like.

A feeling paralleling a slow and gradual death.

I'm not trying to be dramatic.

I'm speaking truthfully.

Every day, you wake up, look at yourself in the mirror, and come to the realization that the person you knew is gradually slipping away.

You watch yourself slowly wither and lose all sense of self.

You desperately want to save yourself, but you can't.

I know exactly what it feels like to want it all to end.

To want my life to end.

To end the feelings of sadness and sorrow.

To end the constant, nauseating feeling of anxiety, panic, and fear.

To end the feeling of being entrapped by my mind.

I know what it feels like to want life to end, to be free of it all, and feel at peace.

I prayed for it almost every day.

But amid all of that despair, I didn't let it end.

I couldn't, and I wouldn't, because there was always something or someone to keep fighting for.

I didn't give up, because of myself, my mom, and my son.

Firstly, I wasn't finished living.

I didn't truly want my life to end.

Even though every day was agonizing, I still had so much to live for.

I didn't want Yalda to be gone.

I didn't want her to leave this world yet.

And my strong faith in God also prevented me from going down that path.

Secondly, I didn't want my life to end, because of my mom.

A woman whose strength in unparalleled.

A woman who has endured more hardship than any other person I've ever known and still continues to be compassionate, loving, and selfless to this day.

My mom, a woman who lost her first-born child to cancer at the age of four, a woman who still stood strong and undefeated as she raised three daughters afterwards.

The thought of giving up on my life meant that she could lose a second child in her lifetime, and I was not ready to impose that pain upon her.

I couldn't inflict that agony on her again.

And lastly, there was my son.

My sweet, beautiful, and amazing little boy.

Despite the illness making me think that I didn't love him, deep down, I did.

I feared for him and his future if I were to end my life.

The fear that for the rest of his life, even if unintentionally, my loved ones would in any way blame him for my life ending.

I didn't want anyone to ever love him less because of it.

It wasn't his fault that I became ill.

But what if someone were to have that thought?

Even the mere thought of it was unimaginable to me.

The thought of anyone ever making him feel that Yalda wasn't there with them because she became a mother to him.

That's what kept me going.

That's what gave me strength and motivation to keep fighting.

So that he would never hear or feel those words.

I had too much to live for, and this illness was not going to take me away from my loved ones and my life.

Even in your lowest moments, in the depths of despair, you need to find your reason to keep going.

Every single one of us has a reason.

No matter how bleak or hopeless it may seem, you have a reason to fight.

Keep fighting.

Mental illness is a long and agonizing road.

But one that you can come back from.

Hopefully this book serves as a way to help you feel connected, shed that sense of loneliness, and help you learn that there is hope for your recovery.

We have commonalities, you and I.

We are fighters.

We are survivors.

We are resilient.

We are courageous.

We are strong.

We are winners.

We are mothers.

3
UNHELPFUL OPINIONS

For so long, I lost my voice.

I allowed the judgements and opinions of others bring me anguish and pain.

I allowed them to hinder my well-being.

There was a voice inside that wanted to escape.

A voice that wanted to express all of the hurt and stand up for myself, but the words couldn't come out.

I didn't have the strength and courage to fight back.

I let the judgement and criticism inside, and as it bottled up, I suffered in return.

I allowed the negative comments and actions toward me build up until I had a massive pile of anger, disappointment, and hurt drowning me.

This illness can render you incapable of using logic and being able to stand up for yourself.

It allows you to be easily manipulated and taken advantage of. You don't have the mental ability, strength, or at times, physical ability to fight back.

When others mistreat you, you desperately want to stand up for yourself but often can't.

Your sense of self-worth and self-love are diminished.

You lose the belief in yourself and what you once stood for.

Your confidence deteriorates, and you quickly succumb to the harsh criticisms and opinions of others, internalizing them and believing them to be true when often, they're not.

You let other people's judgements and perceptions of you skew your own self-perception and confidence.

Don't let yourself get to that point.

That was one of the biggest mistakes I made.

I let the opinions and judgements of others consume me.

I let the cultural pressures defining what was deemed "appropriate behaviour" to stop me from standing up for myself and conducting myself in a way that was best for me, my child, and my family.

Many of us are born into cultures that encourage respecting your elders and living your life by the standard of "what will people think?" Often discouraging a mindset that promotes thinking of yourself first. Therefore, conducting yourself in a manner that is deemed culturally appropriate often prevents individuals from speaking or standing up for themselves.

I let it all hinder my progress and well-being.

I want to help you in stopping that before it advances—or even begins.

I wrote this book to help you find your voice and to help you express what's in your heart so that you or your loved one don't have to suffer the way I did.

Maybe using the strategies that I have outlined in an upcoming chapter will help you regain your voice sooner and fight an easier battle.

As you read my story, I don't want you to ever pity me for what I endured.

Every ounce of me is grateful for this experience because it taught me very important and lifelong lessons.

Sometimes, amazing new beginnings and opportunities arise from the most difficult times, and that's a blessing.

It takes strength, courage, gratitude, and resiliency to overcome such hardships, and those are all qualities to be proud of.

In this chapter, I discuss some of the negative judgements, criticisms, and unhelpful comments that were made toward me—whether to my face or behind my back during the course of my illness.

The intent is not to call out specific individuals; as you will see, I do not mention any names.

However, I intend to explain what feelings and emotions those judgements and comments created within me and how they impacted me during my illness.

It's important to note that the judgements and criticisms made toward you may not be the same as or similar to the ones I faced.

You may be faced with completely different scenarios.

However, the intent of this chapter is to educate you and your support system about the types of criticisms to avoid. I also hope to help you gain your voice back and stand up to such conversations.

∞∞∞

Where to begin?

Let's start with a comment that holds zero truth or scientific validity yet was often directed at me—whether to my face or behind my back.

"Yalda became sick because she didn't want to have kids."

To set the record straight, this criticism was outright false.

In my younger years, prior to planning to have a baby, I wasn't the type of individual who was eager to become a mother.

In fact, I often stated that I never wanted kids.

However, after a few years of being married, my husband and I chose to become parents willingly and planned our pregnancy.

In fact, it actually took us approximately eight months to conceive.

Again, eight months where we willingly chose to have a baby.

So, the comments above, made on multiple occasions, have zero merit or truth to them.

Just because an individual has a specific frame of mind at a certain point in time doesn't mean they are not able to change their minds.

Just because I didn't want kids in my younger years doesn't mean that when the time came for me to have a baby I still held that stance.

People are allowed to change their minds.

We change our perspectives on life all the time.

New experiences, relationships, self-realizations, and a multitude of other reasons can make us alter our thoughts as we progress in life.

So, to assume that I (or any other mother experiencing postpartum mental illness) became ill because of not wanting kids is irresponsible and hurtful.

I also don't think there's any definitive scientific proof to back up such a comment.

I personally know individuals who wanted to become mothers more than anything, yet they still developed postpartum mental illness and even psychosis. And there are also mothers who don't develop postpartum mental illness but still feel a sense of ambivalence about motherhood on occasion.

On the other hand, individuals who didn't want to become mothers both have and haven't developed postpartum mental illness.

The point is that the desire, or lack thereof, to become a mother has no direct correlation on whether or not one develops this ailment.

There are so many other factors, such as your body's hormonal levels, brain's serotonin levels, and genetic predisposition to mental illness, that can contribute to the development of these ailments.

However, wanting or not wanting to become a mother is not one of those factors.

Therefore, to anyone thinking of uttering such words to or about a mother experiencing postpartum mental illness, I urge you to stop and please keep your comments to yourselves.

Unnecessary comments and judgements are hurtful and detrimental to a mother's well-being and ability to heal.

Making such comments doesn't provide her with a needed rationale or justification about why she became ill.

In fact, it does the opposite by compiling an additional layer of hurt, sadness, anger, and guilt upon her that she doesn't need.

It doesn't matter *why* she became ill.

It matters *how* you support her in overcoming the illness and becoming herself again.

Often, people feel that they need to have a reason or justification as to why certain experiences occur in life.

But sometimes, the reason is irrelevant in comparison to the final outcome itself.

So, stay silent, and instead, focus on strategies to support her and help her heal.

This also applies to those of you who are experiencing this illness yourselves.

Stop focusing on why individuals make such comments toward you or silently think them.

The *why* is irrelevant.

Trying to find the rationale behind such thoughts only leads you into a perpetual cycle of anger, hurt, and frustration.

Instead, focus your attention on healing and understanding that you didn't choose to become ill.

Period.

End of story.

∞∞∞

This next comment, which I'm paraphrasing, I found very upsetting. In fact, it made me quite angry.

"Yalda became ill because she didn't want her figure to change. Since she's so into fashion, having a baby altered that, so she's upset now, and it's made her depressed."

Again, an invalid criticism.

Does it seem plausible that women nowadays don't know that their bodies will change during motherhood?

We live in a world surrounded by knowledge, often accessible at our fingertips.

I think not.

That I have a love for fashion is a very truthful comment.

I have loved dressing up, doing my hair and makeup, and looking as fabulous as I want to since I was a child.

I enjoy the creativity that fashion allows me to have, and I embrace it.

I am a huge proponent of looking and feeling confident.

It's just who I am and who I have always been, and I will never apologize for being that way.

However, I am also very well-educated and knowledgeable on human physiology and the biological changes expected during and after pregnancy.

As previously stated, I planned to have a baby. With that came a very clear and transparent understanding that my body would undergo changes as a result.

If I didn't want my body or figure to change, I would not have planned to have a child in the first place.

There are a multitude of other reasons that contribute to a woman's body and shape changing.

Becoming pregnant and having a baby is just one of them.

At the risk of sounding like a broken record, I say this again: wanting or not wanting your body or figure to change is not a valid reason why a mother will or will not develop postpartum mental illness.

I don't dismiss the fact that body image can play a role in impacting a woman's mood or self-perception.

In fact, I wholeheartedly believe in this concept—so much so that my new career and company is devoted to helping break such negative self-perceptions and educating women on how to dress their changing bodies (I will elaborate more on this in the final chapter).

However, what I absolutely do not agree with is the comment that a mother's changing figure or body image is the reason for why she would develop postpartum mental illness. I would say that it may aid in exacerbating the symptoms that are already present, such as lowered self-confidence or mood, but I don't believe that it is *the* cause for why one would develop this ailment in the first place.

I want every mother experiencing this illness to understand that there's not something you did, thought, or said that caused you to become ill.

It's not your fault!

Despite what others may think, you did not choose to become ill, and you most certainly didn't will it with your thoughts about your figure.

You and I are in the statistical category of women who happened to fall prey to this illness, and all we can do is be strong enough to overcome and conquer it.

Don't let the negative perceptions and judgements of others change that.

Don't let their negativity and lack of knowledge impact your confidence and ability to fight for yourself.

You are strong and courageous because you are battling one of the hardest and most difficult experiences in life—all while taking care of a baby.

That is no small feat.

That is what *real* heroes are made of.

Stand up for yourself.

You don't need to be rude or nasty to anyone in doing so.

But you do need to put up clear boundaries when anyone crosses the line and passes incorrect judgements upon you.

You can very eloquently and politely explain that such opinions hold no scientific value and are in fact incorrect.

The rest is up to them to decide whether they choose to believe it or not.

It's taken me many years to come to the realization that people will perceive you how they *want* to perceive you.

Regardless of whether or not their perception is actually factual in nature.

You can be the most "perfect" individual, conducting yourself in the most "perfect" manner, and people will still find fault and judgement within you.

Of course, we all know there is no such thing as real perfection when it comes to humanity.

So, the sooner we all accept that, the sooner we can stop judging one another.

Stop focusing on what others think of you, and focus on what *you* think of yourself.

Opinions are merely that—opinions.

It doesn't mean they're accurate or truthful.

They hold no real power unless you allow them to.

They are the subjective thoughts and feelings others place upon us based on who they are and what they choose to believe.

It doesn't mean they hold any validity.

Stop allowing them to have that level of power over you.

Focus on yourself and your well-being, and do what you need to in order to heal.

The rest is just noise that you can distance yourself from and tune out.

To supporters and individuals surrounding a person experiencing mental illness, I ask you to please think about your comments before making them. Think about whether or not you would appreciate such a comment if the shoe were on the other foot.

If you were in that person's position, how would such judgements or criticisms make you feel?

How would they impact your day-to-day well-being or your ability to function and heal?

Be cognizant of how your opinions and comments can be interpreted, particularly by a mind that has difficulty distinguishing rational comments from irrational ones—a mind that tends to unwillingly and automatically veer toward the negative.

Remember, a depressed and anxious mind doesn't necessarily process information the way our "normal" and healthy minds do.

Comments that may have once been unimpactful or easily debunked may now place a very heavy weight on an individual.

Be kind with your words and actions.

ooooo

Breastfeeding.

A point of contention and a topic that often triggers much debate.

I'll start by saying, it doesn't matter what your stance on breastfeeding is.

Whether you choose to partake in it or not, the decision is solely yours to make.

However, this was one area where I faced severe criticism and judgement because I was unable to breastfeed my son.

In fact, I faced so much judgement that I attribute half of the stress and mental burden that I experienced in the first month and a half of my son's life to breastfeeding issues.

To set the record straight, I was biologically unable to breastfeed my son due to a lack of milk production.

It was not due to a lack of wanting to breastfeed him.

In the first month and a half of his life, I spent my days and nights attached to dual breast pumps in between his formula feedings.

I saw a multitude of lactation consultants during that time.

The last one actually conducted a scientific procedure to measure my milk production and very clearly stated to me and my husband that I physically could not produce enough milk—regardless of all the efforts I was making to breastfeed my son and pump in between.

She reaffirmed what I'd already known the entire time.

However, I can't tell you how many times I was made to feel like I was an inadequate mother and woman because I couldn't breastfeed my son.

I can't tell you how many times I was told that breastfeeding was the healthiest way to feed my baby and that basically, my child would not be healthy because I was formula feeding him.

Take a moment to think about that.

Here I was, a new mother, already feeling the progressing symptoms of postpartum mental illness, and amid all of that, I was made to feel that I wasn't a good enough mother because I couldn't breastfeed my child.

This huge burden and others' judgements were constantly being forced into my head, and I was consistently compared to other new moms who were able to breastfeed their babies.

In fact, I was being met with comments like, "She doesn't want to breastfeed because she doesn't want her breasts to change or become saggy."

This goes back to that same comment about not wanting my figure to change.

Let's discuss this a bit further.

I spent damn near every available moment of my day trying to get my son to breastfeed in order to foster a closeness and bond with him.

Then knowing that he wasn't getting enough milk, I would switch to a bottle with formula.

After he was done feeding, I would change his diaper and put him to sleep.

Then I would proceed to sit and attach myself to dual breast pumps for about forty-five minutes in order to possibly pump more milk.

Repeat, repeat, repeat.

At what point in that sequence could anybody think that breast shape preservation was my goal? Or any mother's goal?

The breast pumping alone was probably sufficient enough to cause my breast shape to change.

If I didn't want to breastfeed my son, I wouldn't have spent so much time attached to the bloody machines every day.

Again, I bring up this topic not to discuss whether breastfeeding is right or wrong.

That's a personal decision that each individual should make on their own.

However, I mention this topic because it's important to understand how unsolicited comments and advice can really help to progress one's stress levels and cause mental distress.

As new mothers, we already have so much to deal with when it comes to having a baby.

Worry, lack of sleep, self-doubt, and the list keeps going.

Couple that with symptoms of depression and the constant berating judgement about how we should or should not conduct ourselves as mothers, and it's a recipe for utter and complete disaster.

In fact, I wholeheartedly believe that my postpartum mental illness progressed and became so much more intense because of all the negative comments that I had to constantly endure.

Every mother is different.

Every individual has their reasons for the way they behave and what they decide is suitable for them and their family.

It is not up to those around them to determine whether they are the right type of mother by comparing them to others. What worked for one may not work for another.

Constant comparisons are detrimental to a new mom's well-being.

Whether these are self-induced comparisons that moms often make themselves or comparisons and judgements made by other individuals.

Just as every child is different and there is no set of rules or guidelines on how they should be parented, the same pertains to new moms.

Yes, there are concepts that may have scientific backing, such as breastfeeding being healthy for one's baby. However, those who typically judge mothers who don't or can't breastfeed are often those who don't have as many issues with breastfeeding. It's very easy to say that it's something all mothers should do when you don't experience problems with it, have adequate or even excess milk production, have no issues with your baby latching on for milk, or any of the multitude of other reasons by which complications and issues arise during breastfeeding. But when you're a woman who biologically just can't produce enough milk, you shouldn't be made to feel that you're a bad mother because your body can't produce enough. The same applies to mothers who have physiological concerns that arise and prevent them from breastfeeding. Those are not fair judgements to place on a mother who probably already feels destroyed by the fact that she can't breastfeed even though she wants to.

There are so many external factors that can play a role in whether or not a mother can, or chooses, to breastfeed.

It is not our place to compare ourselves to other moms, and it is not the place of others to compare us to each other.

The judgements and comparisons need to stop!

ooooo

Moving on to the two comments I heard the most—the ones that many often make the mistake of saying.

"Just think positive thoughts" and "Come on, snap out of it."

Let me explain why these comments are not only unhelpful, but counterproductive to healing.

We have tried to think positively!

Stop asking us to do so!

It's actually quite insulting that people often assume that we are unaware of this concept and that the thought of thinking positively has not occurred to us.

They think it's as though we need someone else to tell us that the magical cure to our anxiety and depression is to suddenly think positive thoughts, and all will be well again.

Please, take a moment to actually think about how that type of comment can be interpreted by someone with mental illness.

It comes across as condescending and insulting.

It feels as though we're being told that we are too incompetent to know that thinking positively will help uplift our moods and calm our minds.

I've mentioned numerous times in this book that an anxious and depressed mind doesn't function the way our "normal" minds do.

However, this does not mean it lacks competence. It just has a harder time rationalizing logic, such as the need to think more positively.

We know that positive thoughts are part of the solution.

However, as I've stated before, our minds can't seem to focus on actually thinking positively, because an anxious and depressed mind more often automatically, and very quickly, veers toward the negative.

We want to think positively.

We've tried numerous times to think positively, but we just can't seem to do so, and when we can, the thoughts don't seem to stick around for long, because the negative ones take over.

When others make comments such as "Just think positive thoughts," it's really defeating.

Not only do we feel defeated by the illness itself, but we then feel belittled and hurt by the fact that our support system and the very people who are supposed to help us feel encouraged are doing the opposite and making us feel inferior and weak instead.

They're making us feel stupid and inadequate by pointing out a concept we're aware of but having a hard time grasping a handle on it.

The same exact concepts apply to the "Come on, snap out of it" comments.

Same thing as before. We understand the concept of it; we have tried and continue to try snapping out of it, but it's not something that can be instantaneously done.

There is no snap moment.

Healing from anxiety and depression doesn't occur at the snap of a finger.

It doesn't occur quickly.

It's often a very long and slow process.

I reiterate, comments such as the ones above are not motivating to those with mental illness; they are condescending and hurtful, and they accomplish the complete opposite of what people often intend them to do.

To draw this chapter to a conclusion, I will mention that there were also numerous instances where I faced criticism regarding the appearance of my home, how often I cooked, whether or not my son had a scheduled routine or not, and so on and so forth.

Firstly, unless someone is present often enough to witness what we go through on a daily basis, they have no right to interfere or comment on our day-to-day lives or decisions.

Even then, they still don't have the right.

My house was typically a disaster, and more often than not, I didn't cook.

To be honest, I was never the "perfect housewife" type of individual to begin with—if such a thing even exists.

I was always someone who focused on my education and career more than mastering cooking and cleaning.

Trust me, my mom tried to instill that in me and my sisters when we were younger—let's be honest, still tries—and is still met with a bit of refusal, at least on my part.

To me, excelling academically and in my career has always meant more.

And I say this with no judgement to those who value the opposite.

There is nothing wrong with valuing a more traditional role in a home.

We each have our own set of values, and there is no right or wrong in that.

However, once I became ill, I was certainly no longer focused on cooking or cleaning.

I did the bare minimum to maintain the hygiene of my home, but often, my house looked cluttered and disorganized.

And that's just the sad truth when it comes to facing mental illness.

When you barely have the motivation to take care of yourself, you need to prioritize things that are important versus those that are not.

To me, keeping my baby alive, taken care of, and trying to survive myself mattered far more than whether or not my house looked immaculate.

Eating the quickest and most convenient meals took precedence over standing in a kitchen, cooking a gourmet meal every day.

Ensuring that my baby survived and was fed, changed, and able to take naps meant more than whether he did all of that at a set time or location.

My mind didn't have the ability to take on those extra tedious steps.

My focus was on survival, and everything else could be put on hold—including my own physical appearance, as I've previously mentioned.

For those of you facing these difficulties right now, one thing I want to highlight is that you don't need to beat yourselves up over it.

At a time when you need to focus on your well-being, keeping an immaculate home or appeasing others shouldn't be your focus or priority.

People will always have their opinions of you—whether they truly understand your motivations or not.

At the end of the day, if you're not well, you can't function well as a mother, partner, daughter, etc.

If you're not well, you can't take care of your baby well enough to help foster the attachment and bond that you need to have.

Your priority must be to focus on getting better so that you can take on your crucial role as a mother.

As I've mentioned before, the point of discussing these topics is to help raise awareness.

I'm not saying that the comments made toward me—or any other mom—were necessarily meant to intentionally cause me hurt or harm.

I'm certain that, in some instances, they were made with some positive intent, and the individuals making them thought they were being helpful.

Who knows?

I'll never really know, and neither will you.

None of us are mind readers.

However, such negative commentary played a tremendous role in making me feel even worse about myself and my incapacitated state of mind.

The best you can do is distance yourself from such negativity and focus your attention toward those who are helping you heal.

Sometimes, relationships will be tested during this process.

However, those who truly care for you will be more understanding and will support your recovery instead of criticizing you.

If someone is offering such harsh criticism toward you, respectfully ask them to stop or distance yourself from them—whether physically or by not engaging in such conversations.

My biggest regret is not stopping these conversations at their onset.

By trying to be respectful and polite, I let people continue to criticize and disrespect me when they didn't truly understand my decisions or what I was going through.

And to be honest, I think some just didn't want to understand.

Instead, I internalized all of that negativity, which in turn exacerbated my symptoms of anxiety and depression.

What I should have done was set very strict boundaries on what I would and would not tolerate.

As I mentioned earlier, postpartum mental illness can render you incapable of standing up for yourself.

Sometimes, you can't set boundaries the way you may have done previously.

I want you to become aware of such scenarios early on and set boundaries before your illness progresses further.

That way, you have a chance at stopping the perpetual negativity before it gets too far.

I wish I had the insight to do that sooner.

I also want you to know that you can, and should, discuss such stressors with your doctor or someone you trust, like a friend or family member.

Someone who is unbiased and objective can help you have honest discussions about the opinions and judgements you're facing and put things into perspective.

This in turn can help you feel more confident in your responses and reduce the amount of stress you succumb to.

They can also help by giving you tips and strategies on how to set those boundaries and stand up for yourself.

Positivity, support, and peace of mind is what you will need to heal.

You need to remove negativity from the equation.

To supporters, I urge you to collectively take a moment to assess the impact of the words that you speak and the actions that you take in such circumstances.

It's perfectly acceptable to offer words of wisdom and advice to your friends and loved ones.

However, I recommend asking them if they are open to receiving the advice first, prior to verbalizing it.

It's a simple gesture.

Ask before speaking.

Not only will this allow you to be met with a more receptive response, but you'll also avoid the risk of hurting the other individual or harming your relationship with them.

None of us will always agree with one another.

We all have different perspectives and points of view.

Instead of focusing on proving that our opinions and perspectives are the right ones, let's focus on being mutually respectful. While we have differing opinions, we can coexist peacefully amid those differences.

Take the time to listen and understand why an individual may be making their decisions; you will often find that their rationale does not come from a malicious or neglectful place.

Sometimes, it's because they have so much stress that certain actions are too difficult to conduct.

That's where you can offer help instead of criticism.

You can help them through the difficulty instead of making them feel inadequate and unworthy.

This will not only help them with healing, but it can strengthen your relationship.

Lastly, it's okay to know that we all make mistakes.

We say and do things that may be hurtful to others.

However, what's important is being accountable for our own words and actions.

If you've ever made similar comments toward someone facing a mental illness—or any hardship—take accountability for it, and understand that it may have been tremendously hurtful to them.

Then take the time to apologize and try to mend the relationship.

Nobody is perfect.

As I said, we all make mistakes.

But where the hurt really happens is when people avoid taking accountability and try to justify or deny their wrongdoings.

It's okay to have differing opinions.

But we can state these differences in either a respectful or malicious manner.

It's up to us to choose which route we take.

Respect, kindness, understanding, and patience will help you navigate these difficult times.

4
STRATEGIES
THAT HELP

Let's veer toward positivity and discuss strategies to help you recover, as well as tips on succeeding for those of you in supportive roles.

I've mentioned this repeatedly: please remember that I am not a medical professional, and I am in no way providing any medical advice.

I can, however, share strategies, tips, and wisdom that I personally used to help me in my recovery.

To ease your reading, I have broken this chapter down into two sections. The first discusses strategies for those currently experiencing mental illness first-hand. The second discusses strategies and tips to aid supporters in their critical roles.

STRATEGIES TO HELP YOURSELF

● *Think of yourself too*

I know that there's an abundance of resources and literature on mental health and methods for self-help.

Although I don't dismiss the usefulness of these sources, my intent is to provide you with a different perspective, using strategies based on my personal experience with these ailments that I believe provide a real and authentic source of hope and strength.

I'm not claiming to be reinventing the wheel, nor will every single strategy that I discuss be a new concept.

However, I feel that the combination of these strategies, some of which may be less-commonly thought of, is what allowed me to recover despite the severity of my symptoms and illness.

Obviously, I can't make any promises or guarantees; however, my hope is that since these strategies worked for me, they may work for you.

First and foremost, I want you to accept that it's okay to make yourself a priority and focus on your own physical and emotional well-being right now.

I know the term *mother* is typically synonymous with *selflessness*.

However, when you are faced with a mental illness that affects your ability to function in the most effective manner, you can't be as helpful to your child if you're not well yourself.

This illness can prevent you from functioning at your best, which can then prevent you from being the best mom that you can be to your child.

This is particularly imperative, as there's quite extensive research on how important attachment is to a child's development.

Attachment theories basically explain how important the child-parent bond is to a child's overall development, even affecting them in adulthood.[7]

Therefore, healing is not only necessary and beneficial for your own well-being, but for the long-term effects it can have on the development of your child.

Stop thinking that focusing on yourself and your well-being is selfish.

It is not!

In fact, I believe it serves quite the opposite.

It allows you to heal and be yourself again, which then gives you the ability to become the mother you desire to be.

To be clear, you must meet your baby's needs in order to help them flourish, but you must also simultaneously help yourself.

Give yourself permission to say, "I am not well."

Give yourself permission to take the necessary time to heal, and stop trying to fight it.

It's okay to admit that you're not well and that you can't do some of the things you used to.

It's okay to adjust your expectations of yourself right now.

It's okay to let the people who are around or supporting you know that you are not well and need additional help.

There is no shame in asking for help.

Just allow yourself to accept all of that. This will allow you to take the steps necessary to work toward healing.

But if you're constantly fighting yourself or those around you and denying your need to heal, then you're only doing yourself a disservice.

You're only hindering your own progress and suffering in silence.

You can't heal or allow others to support you in healing if you can't admit that you are ill and need help in the first place.

Help yourself by being honest with yourself, your doctors, and your support system.

It will go a long way in helping you in your recovery.

● *Write it all down*

One of the most valuable strategies I was encouraged to engage in was to maintain a daily journal of my thoughts and activities.

I must admit, the first few times my doctor suggested this, I was quite resistant.

However, once I actually took her advice and tried it, I realized how beneficial it really was.

The purpose of keeping a daily journal is to write down the tasks or activities you partake in on a daily basis and document your thoughts and feelings.

Why is this so helpful?

Because as I mentioned in earlier chapters, a depressed and anxious mind is often bombarded with competing negative thoughts, and at times, it forgets positive progress or improvements.